The Joy of Christmas

...with songs is as old as Chris-
...ing by the angelic choir over
...of the Child: "Glory to God
...will toward men." To be sure,
... During the first centuries of
...otional hymns, but from the
...the great humanitarian, St.
...ed a more lighthearted, secu-

...day—joy, singing, devotion,
...lio provides abundant mate-
...ng in family groups, schools,
...ianists, organists and guitar-
...tains the best loved carols,
...od number of instrumental
...nts are new and easy to play.

...h Carols suggests "Make we
...ime of Chris-te-mas!"

Distributed throughout the world by Music Sales
257 Park Avenue South, New York, NY10010, U.S.A.

8/9 Frith Street, London W1V 5TZ, England

120 Rothschild Street, Rosebery, N.S.W. 2018, Australia

Printed and bound by J.B. Offset Ltd, Marks Tey, England

Contents

Adeste Fideles . . . . Old Latin Hymn 11
Angels From The Realms Of Glory . Henry Smart 43
Angels We Have Heard On High . . . . French 8
As Lately We Watched . . . . Austrian 33
As With Gladness, Men Of Old . . . . Conrad Kocher 17
Away In A Manger . . . . Luther's Cradle Hymn 7
Behold That Star . . . . Spiritual Carol 16
Birthday Of A King, The . . . . William H. Neidlinger 66
Bring A Torch, Jeannette, Isabella . . . . French 38
Cantique De Noël . . . . Adolphe Adam 62
Carillon On A French Carol . . . . Denes Agay 52
Christ Was Born On Christmas Day . . . . German 41
Christians Awake . . . . John Wainright 50
Christmas Is Coming *Three-Voice Round* . . . . . . Traditional 49
Come All Ye Shepherds . . . . Czech 13
Deck The Halls . . . . Welsh 79
Ding-Dong Merrily On High . . . . French 15
First Noël, The . . . . Traditional 34
Friendly Beasts, The . . . . English 31
From Heaven High I Come To You . . . . Martin Luther 53
Fum, Fum, Fum . . . . Spanish 23
Gesù Bambin . . . . Italian 32
Go Tell It On The Mountain . . . . Spiritual Carol 10
God Be With You . . . . Swiss 19
God Bless All *Two-Voice Round* . . . . Traditional 69
God Rest You Merry, Gentlemen . . . . English 24
Golden Carol, The . . . . English 18
Good Christian Men, Rejoice . . . . German 20
Good King Wenceslas . . . . Latin Spring Carol 12
Hark! The Herald Angels Sing . . Felix Mendelssohn-Bartholdy 42
Hear The Angel Voices *Two-Voice Round* . . . . . Hungarian 56
Here We Come A-Caroling . . . . English Wassail Song 36
Holly And The Ivy, The . . . . English 26
I Heard The Bells On Christmas Day . . . . J. Baptiste Colkin 21
I Saw Three Ships . . . . English 25
I Wonder As I Wander . . . . Appalachian Carol 51
In Dulci Jubilo . . . . German 20
It Came Upon The Midnight Clear . . . . . . Richard S. Willis 9
Jesus Was Born To Mary . . . . Italian 32

Jingle Bells . . . . James Pierpont 5
Jolly Old Saint Nicholas . . . . Traditional 5
Joy To The World . . . . Georg Friedrich Händel
Lo, How A Rose . . . . Michael Praetorius 3
Lullaby Carol . . . . Polish 2
Luther's Cradle Hymn
March Of The Three Kings . . . . Provencal Melody 4
Masters In This Hall . . . . French-English 2
Night Of Nights . . . . Mendelssohn-Agay 7
O Christmas Tree . . . . German 3
O Come All Ye Faithful . . . . Old Latin Hymn 11
O Come Little Children . . . . Johann A. P. Schulz 6
O Holy Night . . . . Adolphe Adam 6
O Little Town Of Bethlehem . . . . Lewis H. Redner
Oh, How Joyfully . . . . Sicilian Hymn 1
O Saviour Sweet . . . . Johann Sebastian Bach 5
O Sanctissima . . . . Sicilian Hymn 1
O Tannenbaum . . . . German 3
Old French Carol . . . . César Franck 6
Pastorale *from the "Christmas Concerto"* . . Arcangelo Corelli 7
Pat-A-Pan . . . . French 2
Rejoice And Be Merry . . . . English 5
Rise Up, Shepherd, And Follow . . . . Spiritual Carol 4
Serenade To The Holy Family *theme from the oratorio*
"The Childhood of Christ" . . . . Hector Berlioz 7
Silent Night . . . . Franz Gruber
Sing, Shepherds! . . . . Hungarian 3
Slumber Song Of The Infant Jesus . . . . . . François Gevaert 2
Swiss Noël . . . . Louis-Claude Daquin 7
Twelve Days Of Christmas, The . . . . English 4
Up On The Housetop . . . . Traditional 6
Vieux Noël . . . . César Franck 6
Virgin's Lullaby, The . . . . Dudley Buck 6
We Three Kings Of Orient Are . . . John Henry Hopkins, Jr. 4
We Wish You A Merry Christmas . . . . English 8
While Shepherds Watched Their Flocks
. . . . Georg Friedrich Händel 3
Willie, Bring Your Little Drum . . . . French 2

Joy To The World

Isaac Watts

Georg Friedrich Händel

2. Joy to the world! the Saviour reigns;
Let men their songs employ;
While fields and floods, rocks, hills and plains
Repeat the sounding joy,
Repeat the sounding joy,
Repeat, repeat the sounding joy.

3. He rules the world with truth and grace,
And makes the nations prove
The glories of His righteousness,
And wonders of His love,
And wonders of His love,
And wonders, and wonders of His Love.

Silent Night

The original version as copied from the composer's manuscript

Franz Gruber

Moderato

Si - lent night! Ho - ly night!

All___ is calm, All___ is bright, 'Round yon vir - gin

moth - er and Child! Ho - ly in - fant, so ten - der and mild,

Sleep___ in heav - en - ly peace, _____ Sleep___ in heav - en - ly

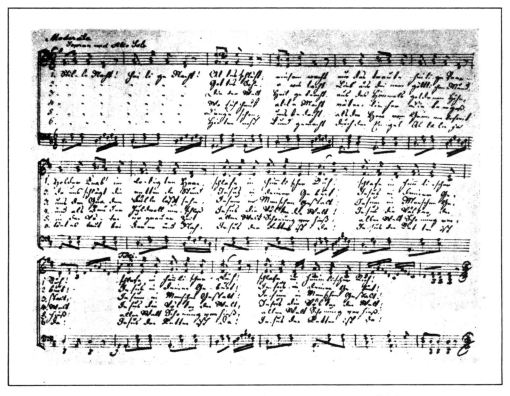

Manuscript of an arrangement by Franz Gruber, in his hand, in the Salzburg Museum

O Little Town Of Bethlehem

Phillips Brooks

Lewis H. Redner

3. How silently, how silently,
   The wondrous gift is giv'n!
   So God imparts to human hearts
   The blessing of his heav'n.
   No ear may hear His coming,
   But in this world of sin,
   Where meek souls will receive Him still,
   The dear Christ enters in.

4. O Holy Child of Bethlehem!
   Descend to us, we pray;
   Cast out our sin, and enter in;
   Be born in us today.
   We hear the Christmas angels
   The great glad tidings tell;
   O come to us abide with us,
   Our Lord Emmanuel.

Away In A Manger

Luther's Cradle Hymn

1. A-way in a man-ger, no crib for a bed, The

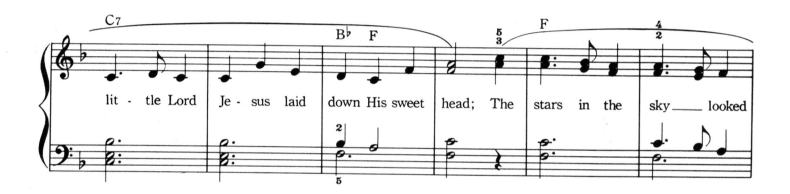

lit-tle Lord Je-sus laid down His sweet head; The stars in the sky___ looked

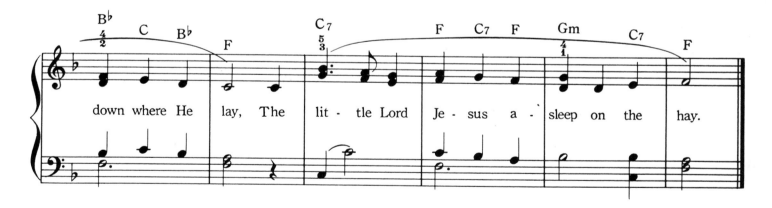

down where He lay, The lit-tle Lord Je-sus a-sleep on the hay.

2. The cattle are lowing,
   The poor Baby wakes,
   But little Lord Jesus
   No crying He makes;
   I love Thee Lord Jesus,
   Look down from the sky,
   And stay by my cradle
   Till morning is nigh.

3. Be near me, Lord Jesus,
   I ask Thee to stay
   Close by me forever,
   And love me, I pray;
   Bless all the dear children
   In Thy tender care,
   And take us to heaven
   To live with Thee there.

Angels We Have Heard On High

French

3. Come to Bethlehem and see
   Him whose birth the angels sing;
   Come adore on bended knee
   Christ, the Lord, the new-born King.
   Refrain:

4. See Him in a manger laid,
   Whom the choir of angels praise;
   Holy Spirit, lend thine aid,
   While our hearts in love we raise.
   Refrain:

It Came Upon The Midnight Clear

Edmund H. Sears

Richard S. Willis

2. Still through the cloven skies they come,
   With peaceful wings unfurled,
   And still their heav'nly music floats
   O'er all the weary world;
   Above its sad and lowly plains
   They bend on hov'ring wing,
   And ever o'er its Babel sounds
   The blessed angels sing.

3. For lo! the days are hast'ning on,
   By prophets seen of old,
   When with the evercircling years,
   Shall come the time foretold,
   When the new heav'n and earth shall own
   The Prince of Peace their King,
   And the whole world send back the song
   Which now the angels sing.

Go Tell It On The Mountain

Spiritual Carol

O Come All Ye Faithful

Adeste Fideles

English words by
Frederick Oakley

Old Latin Hymn

With steady motion

O come, all ye faith-full, Joy-ful and tri-umph-ant, O come ye, O come ye to Beth-le-hem. Come and be-hold Him Born the King of an-gels: O come, let us a-dore Him, O come let us a-dore Him, O come let us a-dore Him, Christ the Lord.

2. Sing, choirs of angels, sing in exultation,
O sing, all ye citizens of heaven above!
Glory to God, all Glory in the highest; *Refrain:*

3. Yea, Lord, we greet Thee, born this happy morning,
Jesus, to Thee be all glory giv'n;
World of the Father, Now in flesh appearing; *Refrain:*

5 verses

Good King Wenceslas

John Mason Neale

Latin Spring Carol
(16th Century)

2. "Hither, page, and stand by me,
   If thou know'st it, telling,
   Yonder peasant, who is he?
   Where and what his dwelling?"
   "Sire, he lives a good league hence,
   Underneath the mountain;
   Right against the forest fence,
   By St. Agnes fountain!"

3. "Bring me flesh and bring me wine,
   Bring me pinelogs hither;
   Thou and I will see him dine
   When we bear them hither."
   Page and monarch forth they went,
   Forth they went together
   Thro' the rude wind's wild lament
   And the bitter weather.

4. "Sire, the night is darker now,
   And the wind grows stronger;
   Fails my heart, I know not how,
   I can go no longer."
   "Mark my footsteps, my good page,
   Tread thou in them boldly,
   Thou shalt find the winter's rage
   Freeze thy blood less coldly!"

5. In his master's steps he trod,
   Where the snow lay dinted;
   Heat was in the very sod
   Which the Saint had printed;
   Therefore, Christian men, be sure,
   Wealth or rank possessing,
   Ye who now will bless the poor,
   Shall yourselves find blessing.

Come, All Ye Shepherds

Czech

2. Come hear what wonderful tidings are fraught.
   In Bethlehem see what joy they have brought.
   Good will from heaven to man is given,
   Peace never ending to earth descending,
   Glory to God!

3. Haste then to Bethlehem, there to behold
   Jesus the Babe of whom angels have told.
   There to His glory tell we the story,
   Glad voices raising Him over praising,
   Hallelujah!

Oh, How Joyfully

O Sanctissima

Sicilian Hymn

With spirited motion

2. Oh, how joyfully,
   Oh, how merrily
   Christmas comes with its
     grace divine!
   Peace on earth is reigning,
   Christ our peace regaining,
   Hail, ye Christians,
   Hail the joyous Christmas time!

3. Oh, how joyfully,
   Oh, how merrily
   Christmas comes with its
     life divine!
   Angels high in glory
   Chant the Christmas story,
   Hail, ye Christians,
   Hail the joyous Christmas time!

Ding-Dong Merrily On High

French

3. Praise Him! people far and near,
   And join the angels' singing.
   Ding, dong, everywhere we hear
   The Christmas bells a-ringing.
   Refrain:

4. Hear them ring this happy morn!
   Our God a gift has given;
   Ding, dong, Jesus Christ is born!
   A precious Child from heaven.
   Refrain:

Behold That Star

Spiritual Carol

As With Gladness, Men Of Old

William Dix

Conrad Kocher

3. As they offered gifts most rare
   At that manger rude and bare,
   So may we with holy joy,
   Pure and free from sin's alloy,
   All our costliest treasures bring,
   Christ, to Thee, our heav'nly King.

4. Holy Jesus, every day
   Keep us in the narrow way;
   And, when earthly things are past,
   Bring our ransomed souls at last
   Where they need no star to guide,
   Where no clouds Thy glory hide.

The Golden Carol

2. Oh! ever thought be of His name
   On Christmas in the morning,
   Who bore for us both grief and shame
   Affliction's sharpest scorning.
   And may we die when death shall come,
   On Christmas in the morning,
   And see in heav'n our glorious home,
   That star of Christmas morning.

God Be With You

Moderately slow

Swiss

2. Last night the shepherds in the East
   Saw many wondrous things,
   Saw many wondrous things,
   The Christmas star shone from afar,
   And joyous angels sang for Him.

   The blessed day has come,
   The day that Christ is born,
   Oh praise His name above,
   And look to Him in love.
   'Tis Jesus' birth, sing, all the earth!
   Laud Him this happy Christmas morn.

Good Christian Men, Rejoice

In Dulci Jubilo

John M. Neale

German (14th Century)

2. Good Christian men, rejoice
With heart and soul and voice;
Now ye hear of endless bliss:
Joy! Joy!
Jesus Christ was born for this!
He hath oped the heav'nly door,
And man is blessed evermore;
Christ was born for this!
Christ was born for this!

3. Good Christian men, rejoice
With heart and soul and voice;
Now ye need not fear the grave:
Peace! Peace!
Jesus Christ is born to save!
Calls you one and calls you all
To gain His everlasting hall;
Christ was born to save!
Christ was born to save!

I Heard The Bells On Christmas Day

Henry W. Longfellow

J. Baptiste Colkin

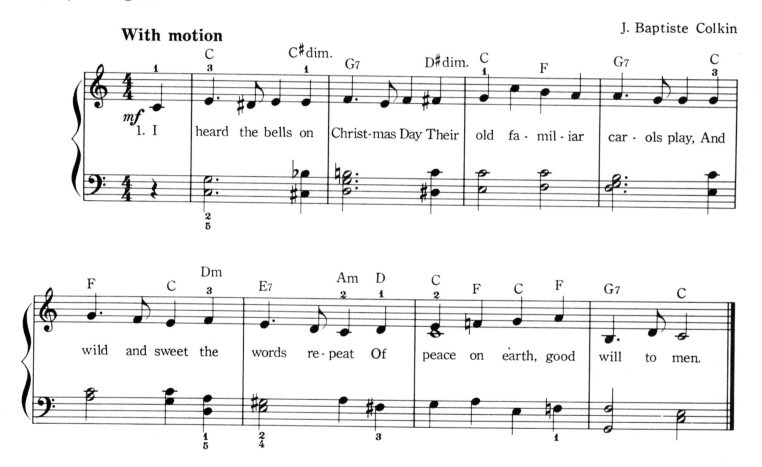

2. I thought how, as the day had come,
The belfries of all Christendom
Had rolled along th' unbroken song
Of peace on earth, good will to men.

4. Then pealed the bells more loud and deep,
God is not dead, nor doth He sleep;
The wrong shall fail, the right prevail,
With peace on earth, good will to men.

3. And in despair I bowed my head,
"There is no peace on earth," I said,
" For hate is strong, and mocks the song
Of peace on earth, good will to men."

5. Till, ringing, singing on its way,
The world revolv'd from night to day,
A voice, a chime, a chant sublime,
Of peace on earth good will to men.

Lullaby Carol

Polish

Fum, Fum, Fum

Moderately, with marked rhythm

Spanish

2. Thanks to God for holidays, sing fum, fum, fum.
    Thanks to God for holidays, sing fum, fum, fum.
    Now we all our voices raise — And sing a song of grateful
        praise,
    Celebrate in song and story, all the wonders of his glory,
    Fum, fum, fum.

God Rest You Merry, Gentlemen

English

2. From God our heavenly Father
A blessed angel came;
And unto certain shepherds
Brought tidings of the same;
How that in Bethlehem was born
The Son of God by name. *Refrain:*

3. Now to the Lord sing praises,
All you within this place,
And with true love and brotherhood
Each other now embrace;
This holy tide of Christmas
All others doth deface. *Refrain.*

I Saw Three Ships

English

3. The Virgin Mary and Christ was there,
On Christmas Day, on Christmas Day.
The Virgin Mary and Christ was there,
On Christmas Day in the morning.

4. Then let us all rejoice amain,
On Christmas Day, on Christmas Day,
Then let us all rejoice amain,
On Christmas day in the morning.

The Holly And The Ivy

English

3. The holly bears a berry
   As red as any blood,
   And Mary bore sweet Jesus Christ,
   To do poor sinners good:
   Refrain:

4. The holly bears a prickle,
   As sharp as any thorn,
   And Mary bore sweet Jesus Christ
   On Christmas day in the morn:
   Refrain:

Masters In This Hall
A Christmas Processional

Spirited walking tempo

French - English

2. Then to Bethl'em town
   We went two and two,
   In a sorry place
   We heard the oxen low:
   Refrain:

3. Ox and ass Him know
   Kneeling on their knee
   Wond'rous joy and I
   This little Babe to see:
   Refrain:

4. This is the Christ, the Lord,
   Masters be ye glad!
   Christmas is come in
   And no folk should be sad:
   Refrain:

Pat - A - Pan
Willie, Bring Your Little Drum

French

2. When the men of olden days
   To the King of Kings gave praise,
   On the fife and drum did play,
   Tu-re-lu-re-lu,
   Pat-a-pat-a-pan,
   On the fife and drum did play,
   So their hearts were glad and gay!

3. God and man today became
   More in tune than fife and drum,
   So be merry while you play,
   Tu-re-lu-re-lu,
   Pat-a-pat-a-pan,
   So be merry while you play,
   Sing and dance this Christmas day!

Slumber Song Of The Infant Jesus

François Gevaert

2. Mid lilies white and roses red,
Sleep, sleep, in Thy lowly bed,
All the cherubim, etc.

3. While gentle shepherds knee in prayer,
Sleep, sleep, my Child so fair.
All the cherubim, etc.

Lo, How A Rose

Michael Praetorius

Moderately, with tenderness

The Friendly Beasts

Moderately

English (12th Century)

3. "I", said the cow all white and red,
   "I gave him my manger for his bed,
   I gave him my hay to pillow his head",
   "I", said the cow all white and red.

4.. "I", said the sheep with curly horn,
   "I gave him my wool for his blanket warm;
   He wore my coat on Christmas morn".
   "I" said the sheep with curly horn.

5. "I", said the dove from the rafters high,
   "Cooed him to sleep that he should not cry,
   We cooed him. to sleep, my mate and I",
   "I", said the dove from the rafters high.

6. Thus every beast by some good spell,
   In the stable dark was glad to tell
   Of the gift he gave Emanuel,
   The gift he gave Emanuel.

Gesù Bambin
Jesus Was Born To Mary

Italian

2. In Bethlehem's rude stable,
   There in the cattle stall,
   Joseph and Mary by Him,
   Christ came to save us all.

He came to save us all,
The star shone bright above Him;
We honor Him and love Him,
This little holy Child, this little holy Child.

As Lately We Watched

Austrian

3. His throne is a manger, His court is a loft,
But troops of bright angels, in lay, sweet and soft,
Him they proclaim, our Christ by name,
And earth, sky, and air, straight are filled with His fame.

4. Then shepherds, be joyful, salute your liege King,
Let hills and dales ring to the song that ye sing,
Blest be the hour, welcome the morn,
For Christ our dear Saviour on earth now is born.

The First Noël

Traditional

3. This star drew nigh to the Northwest,
   O'er Bethlehem it took its rest,
   And there it did both stop and stay,
   Right over the place where Jesus lay.
   Chorus:

4. Then entered in those wisemen three,
   Full rev'rently upon their knee,
   And offered there in His presence,
   Their gold and myrrh and frankincense.
   Chorus:

Sing, Shepherds!

Lively and gay

Hungarian

Sing, shep-herds, be mer-ry, lift your voic - es!

Born is a King and the world re-joic - es.

Sing out the news, shout from ev-'ry stee - ple:

"Born is the Sa-viour of all the peo - ple."

Here We Come A-Caroling

English Wassail Song

2. We are not daily beggars
That beg from door to door
But we are neighbor's children,
Whom you have seen before.
Refrain:

3. God bless the Master of this house,
Likewise the Mistress too;
And all the little children
That round the table go.
Refrain:

O Christmas Tree

O Tannenbaum

German

2. ‖:O Christmas Tree, O Christmas Tree,
   Thy message is enduring;:‖
   So long ago in Bethlehem
   Was born the Saviour of all men;
   O Christmas Tree, O Christmas Tree,
   Thy message is enduring.

3. ‖:O Christmas Tree, O Christmas Tree,
   Thy faith is so unchanging;:‖
   A symbol sent from God above,
   Proclaiming Him the Lord of Love;
   O Christmas Tree, O Christmas Tree,
   How true you stand unchanging!

Bring A Torch, Jeannette, Isabella

French

While Shepherds Watched Their Flocks

Georg Friedrich Händel

2. "Fear not!" said He, for mighty dread
   Had seized their troubled mind,
   "Glad tidings of great joy I bring,
   To you and all mankind,
   To you and all mankind."

3. "To you, in David's town, this day
   Is born of David's line
   The Savior who is Christ the Lord,
   And this shall be the sign,
   And this shall be the sign."

4. "The Heav'nly Babe you there shall find
   To human view displayed,
   All meanly wrapped in swathing band
   And in a manger laid,
   And in a manger laid."

5. "All glory be to God on high,
   And to the earth be peace,
   Good will henceforth from heav'n to men,
   Begin and never cease,
   Begin and never cease!"

We Three Kings Of Orient Are

John Henry Hopkins, Jr.

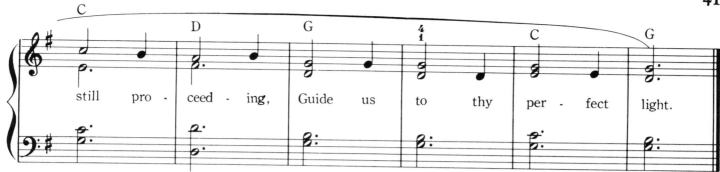

still pro - ceed - ing, Guide us to thy per - fect light.

2. Born a King on Bethlehem plain,
Gold I bring to crown Him again,
King forever, Ceasing never
Over us all to reign. *Refrain:*

3. Frankincense to offer have I,
Incense owns a Deity night:
Prayer and praising, All men raising,
Worship Him, God on high. *Refrain:*

4. Myrrh is mine; its bitter perfume
Breathes a life of gathering gloom;
Sorrowing, sighing, Bleeding, dying,
Sealed in the stone cold tomb. *Refrain:*

5. Glorious now behold Him arise,
King and God, and sacrifice;
Heaven sings Alleluia:
Alleluia the earth replies. *Refrain:*

Christ Was Born On Christmas Day

Rather bright

German

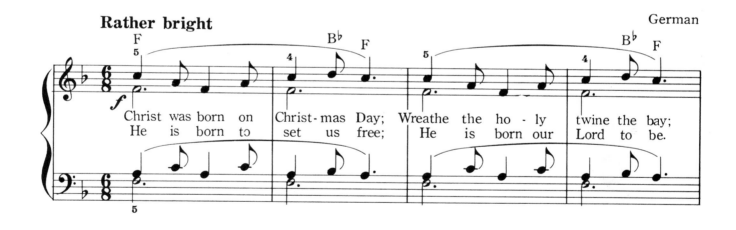

Christ was born on Christ-mas Day; Wreathe the ho - ly twine the bay;
He is born to set us free; He is born our Lord to be.

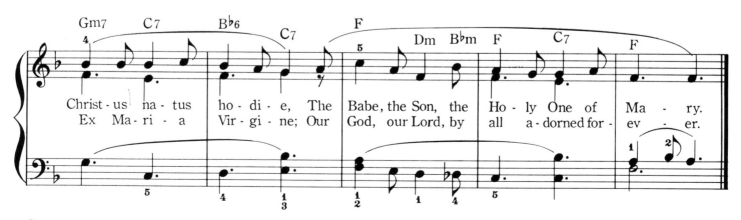

Christ-us na - tus ho - di - e, The Babe, the Son, the Ho - ly One of Ma - ry.
Ex Ma-ri - a Vir - gi - ne; Our God, our Lord, by all a-dorned for - ev - er.

Hark! The Herald Angels Sing

Charles Wesley

Felix Mendelssohn-Bartholdy

2. Christ, by highest heaven adored;
Christ, the everlasting Lord;
Come, Desire of Nations, come,
Fix in us thy humble home.
Veiled in flesh the Godhead see;
Hail th'Incarnate Deity,
Pleased as man with man to dwell;
Jesus, our Emmanuel; *Refrain:*

3. Hail, the heavenborn Prince of Peace!
Hail, the Sun of Righteousness!
Light and life to all He brings,
Risen with healing in His wings;
Mild He lays His glory by,
Born that man no more may die,
Born to raise the sons of earth,
Born to give them second birth; *Refrain:*

Angels From The Realms Of Glory

James Montgomery

Henry Smart

2. Shepherds, in the fields abiding,
Watching o'er your flocks by night,
God with man is now residing,
Yonder shines the infant Light:
Come and worship, Come and worship,
Worship Christ, the newborn King!

3. Sages, leave your contemplations,
Brighter visions beam afar;
Seek the great Desire of nations;
Ye have seen His natal star:
Come and worship, Come and worship,
Worship Christ, the newborn King!

March Of The Three Kings

Provencal Melody

Here they come, let's meet the grand pa - rade Of three great kings— who come proud - ly march - ing;— Here they come, let's meet them on the way, The three great kings— in their fine ar - ray. They come with pa - ges all dressed in gold, And hun - dred guards with— shin - ing— ar - mor, The flags are wav - ing, the church bell rings, Let's march to - geth - er with the three great kings.

The Twelve Days Of Christmas

English

Two—tur-tle doves, and a par-tridge—in a pear tree.

6. On the sixth day of Christ-mas, my true love gave to me six geese a-lay-ing,
7. On the seventh day of Christ-mas, my true love gave to me seven swans a-swim-ming,
8. On the eighth day of Christ-mas, my true love gave to me eight maids a-milk-ing,
9. On the ninth day of Christ-mas, my true love gave to me nine la-dies wait-ing,
10. On the tenth day of Christ-mas, my true love gave to me ten lords a-leap-ing,
11. On the eleventh day of Christ-mas, my true love gave to me 'lev-en pip-ers pip-ing,
12. On the twelfth day of Christ-mas, my true love gave to me twelve drummers drumming.

Five gold-en rings; Four—mock-ing birds, Three french hens,

Two—tur-tle doves, and a par-tridge—in a pear tree. tree.

* Repeat this measure as often as necessary, so that these lines may be sung in reverse order, each time ending with "Six geese a laying."

Rise Up, Shepherd, And Follow

Spiritual Carol

Christmas Is Coming

Three - Voice Round

Christians Awake

John Byron

John Wainright

2. Then to the watchful shepherds it was told,
Who heard th'angelic herald's voice: "Behold,
I bring good tidings of a Saviour's birth
To you and all the nations upon earth;
This day hath God fulfilled His promised word,
This day is born a Saviour, Christ, the Lord.

3. He spake, and straightway the celestial choir,
In hymns of joy, unknown before conspire:
The praises of redeeming love they sang,
And heav'n's whole arch with Alleluias rang,
God's highest glory was their anthem still,
Peace upon earth, and unto men good will.

I Wonder As I Wander

Slowly, freely

Appalachian Carol

1. I wonder as I wander, out under the sky How Jesus the Saviour did come for to die; To save lowly people like you and like I, I wonder as I wander out under the sky.

2. When Jesus was born, it was in a cow's stall,
   With shepherds and wise men and angels and all.
   The blessings of Christmas from heaven did fall,
   And the weary world woke to the Saviour's call.

Carillon On A French Carol

Il est né, le divin enfant

Denes Agay

From Heaven High I Come To You

Martin Luther

Our praise to God in heaven high,
This little Child we glorify.
Let us all be of goodly cheer
And hail with joy the bright New Year!

Rejoice And Be Merry

English

2. A heavenly vision appeared in the sky;
   Vast numbers of angels the shepherds did spy,
   Proclaiming the birthday of Jesus our King,
   Who brought us salvation His praises we'll sing!

3. Likewise a bright star in the sky did appear,
   Which led the Wise Men from the east to draw near;
   They found the Messiah, sweet Jesus our King,
   Who brought us salvation His praises we'll sing!

O Saviour Sweet

Johann Sebastian Bach

Gently moving

2. O Saviour meek, O Saviour mild,
   Who came a happy Christmas Child,
   Good will and peace and heavenly light
   Came to all men that blessed night.
   O Saviour meek, O Saviour mild.

3. O God of grace, O God of love,
   Thy blessings send us from above;
   Protect us from all earthly strife,
   And guide us to Thy perfect Life.
   O God of grace, O God of love.

Hear The Angel Voices

Two - Voice Round

Hungarian

Moderately

Hear the an - gel voi - ces sing - ing "Glo - ri - a! A

Child is born in Beth - le - hem, Hal - le - lu - jah!" Let us

see Him in His hum - ble man - ger lie, Let us

greet Him, glo - ry to our Lord on high!

Jolly Old Saint Nicholas

Traditional

2. When the clock is striking twelve,
   When I'm fast asleep,
   Down the chimney broad and black,
   With your pack you'll creep;
   All the stockings you will find
   Hanging in a row;
   Mine will be the shortest one,
   You'll be sure to know.

3. Johnny wants a pair of skates;
   Susy wants a dolly;
   Nellie wants a story book;
   She thinks dolls are folly;
   As for me, my little brain
   Isn't very bright;
   Choose for me, Old Santa Claus,
   What you think is right.

Jingle Bells

James Pierpont

Lively

Dash-ing thro' the snow In a one-horse o-pen sleigh;

O'er the fields we go, Laugh-ing all the way.

Bells on bob-tail ring, Mak-ing spi-rits bright, What

fun it is to ride and sing A sleigh-ing song to night!

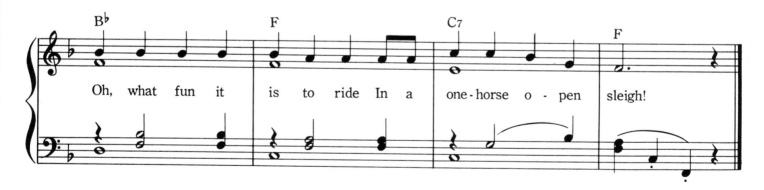

2. Day or two ago
I thought I'd take a ride,
Soon Miss Fanny Bright
Was seated at my side.
The horse was lean and lank,
Misfortune seem'd his lot,
He got into a drifted bank,
And we, we got upsot!
Refrain:

3. Now the ground is white,
Go it while you're young!
Take the girls tonight,
And sing this sleighing song.
Just get a bobtail'd bay,
Twoforty for his speed,
Then hitch him to an open sleigh
And crack! You'll take the lead.
Refrain:

Up On The Housetop

Traditional

2. First comes the stocking of little Nell;
   Oh, dear Santa, fill it well;
   Give her a dollie that laughs and cries,
   One that will open and shut her eyes.
   Refrain:

3. Next comes the stocking of little Will;
   Oh, just see what a glorious fill;
   Here is a hammer and lots of tacks,
   Also a ball and a whip that cracks.
   Refrain:

O Come Little Children

Johann A. P. Schulz

2. The hay is His pillow, the manger His bed,
   The beasts stand in wonder to gaze on His head,
   Yet there where He lieth, so weak and so poor,
   Come shepherds and wise men to kneel at His door.

3. Now "Glory to God!" sing the angels on high,
   And "Peace upon earth!" heavn'ly voices reply.
   Then come, little children, and join in the lay
   That gladdened the world on that first Christmas Day.

O Holy Night

Cantique De Noël

Adolphe Adam

The Virgin's Lullaby

Dudley Buck

The Birthday Of A King

William H. Neidlinger

Old French Carol
Vieux Noël

César Franck

God Bless All

Two-Voice Round

Traditional

Merrily

God bless all good friends here, A

mer-ry, mer-ry Christ-mas and a Hap-py New Year!

ending

repeat ad lib.

Serenade To The Holy Family

Theme from the Oratorio "The Childhood Of Christ"

Hector Berlioz

D.C. al Fine

Pastorale

from the "Christmas Concerto"

Arcangelo Corelli

Night Of Nights
(Based on a Theme by Mendelssohn)

Words and adaptation by
Denes Agay and Sylvia Eversole

Night of nights! In calm splen-dor

dream-ing lay all the earth be-neath a

sky___ filled with light; Shep-herds saw a

child _____ sent from a - bove _____ to lead the world _____ A - way from

cresc.

dark - ness and des - pair, A Child, a

crescendo

f marcato

ho - - ly Child! Oh ___ won - drous night of

f

nights! In gen - tle love the shep - herds

p

cresc.

p

crescendo

bowed be - fore the Babe who lay sleep - ing,

Soft sleep - ing, That bles - sed

night, That won - drous, ho - ly night of nights!

oh night of nights.

Swiss Noël

Louis-Claude Daquin

Deck The Halls

Welsh

2. See the blazing Yule before us,
   Fa-la-la-la-la, la-la-la-la.
   Strike the harp and join the chorus,
   Fa-la-la-la-la, la-la-la-la.
   Follow me in merry measure,
   Fa-la-la, la-la la, la-la-la.
   While I tell of Yuletide treasure,
   Fa-la-la-la-la, la-la-la-la.

3. Fast away the old year passes,
   Fa-la-la-la-la, la-la-la-la.
   Hail the new, ye lads and lasses,
   Fa-la-la-la-la, la-la-la-la.
   Sing we joyous all together,
   Fa-la-la, la-la la, la-la-la.
   Heedless of the wind and weather.
   Fa-la-la-la-la, la-la-la-la.

We Wish You A Merry Christmas

English

2. Oh, bring us some figgy pudding,
   Oh, bring us some figgy pudding,
   Oh, bring us some figgy pudding,
   And bring it out here! *Chorus:*

3. We won't go until we got some,
   We won't go until we got some,
   We won't go until we got some,
   So bring some out here. *Chorus:*

9/94 (18718)